It was an exciting time of discovery in the world. Things people had only dreamed about were being invented—including flying machines.

The boy would grow up to be a pilot. He would write about courageous flights, but also about places you might find if you were to fly long enough and far enough. What did he find on the earth? What did he find in the sky?

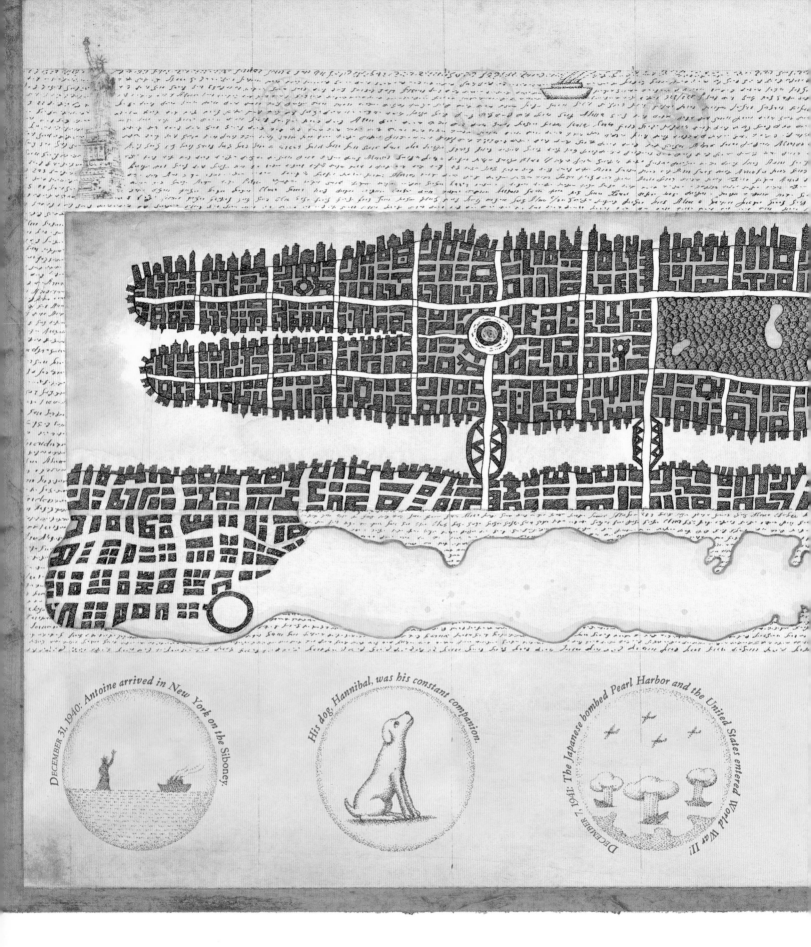

He spent his first year in the United States writing Flight to Arras.

Antoine found New York overwhelming. He didn't speak English and felt out of place, no longer flying but endlessly contemplating the direction the world was taking.

Antoine's wife joined him and for a while they lived on Central Park South.

A book about a war pilot, it was one of the most popular books of the year!

FLIGHT TO ARRAS

Published February 1942

He worked on The Little Prince at the Bevin House on Long Island.

He sent an inscribed copy to President Roosevelt expressing his thanks: "For President Franklin Roosevelt, whose country is taking on the heavy burden of saving the world."

He thought back to his childhood, the places he had seen, the things he had done, and the people he had met. He bought a small box of watercolor paints and started working on an illustrated book about a boy with golden hair.

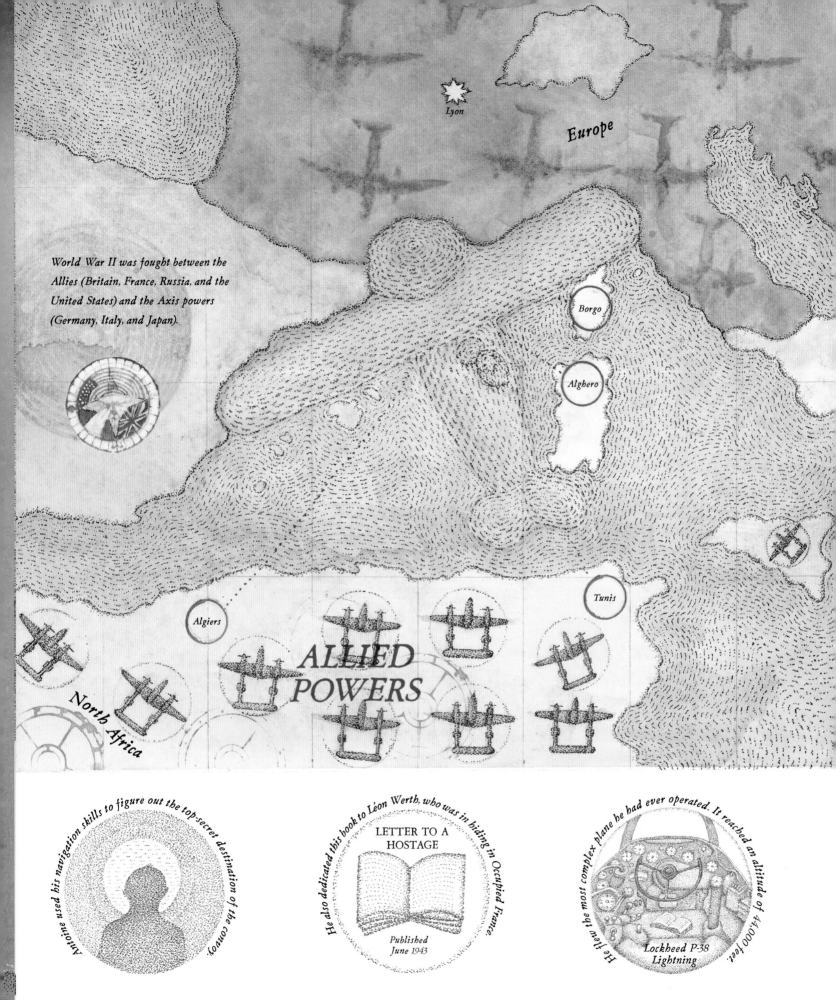

Lyon

Europe

World War II was fought between the
Allies (Britain, France, Russia, and the
United States) and the Axis powers
(Germany, Italy, and Japan).

Borgo

Alghero

Tunis

Algiers

ALLIED
POWERS

North Africa

Antoine used his navigation skills to figure out the top-secret destination of the convoy.

He also dedicated this book to Léon Werth, who was in hiding in Occupied France.

LETTER TO A
HOSTAGE

Published
June 1943

He flew the most complex plane he had ever operated. It reached an altitude of 44,000 feet.

Lockheed P-38
Lightning

The 2/33 Reconnaissance Group was now part of the Allied forces.

Antoine joined his old squadron in North Africa. He asked for flights that
would send him over southern France, where his family was living.

AXIS POWERS

The 2/33 Reconnaissance Group was part of the Mediterranean Allied Photo Reconnaissance Wing (MAPRW), made up of British, American, and French pilots. Antoine flew with them from June to August 1943, when he was grounded for crashing a plane on the runway, and then rejoined them in May 1944.

ANTOINE DE SAINT-EXUPÉRY'S

COMPLETED MISSIONS:

7/21/43: From Tunis over southern France

6/14/44: From Alghero over the Rodez region

6/23/44: From Alghero over southern France

6/29/44: From Alghero over southern France

7/11/44: From Alghero over the Alps

7/14/44: From Alghero over Annecy region

7/18/44: From Borgo over the Alps

Mediterranean Sea

He continued his habit of reading while flying, even when wearing an oxygen mask.

Antoine missed his forty-fourth birthday party, prepared by the 2/33, because of engine trouble.

He kept the manuscript of The Wisdom of the Sands with him wherever he went.

They first flew from Algiers. Then, as more cities were liberated, they moved closer to France.

On July 31, 1944, at 8:45 a.m., he took off from Borgo, Corsica, to photograph enemy positions east of Lyon. It was a beautiful day. He was due back at 12:30.

But he never returned. Some say he forgot his oxygen mask and vanished at sea.

Maybe Antoine found his own glittering planet next to the stars.